COLORING BOOKS
FOR TEENS
OCEAN DESIGNS

ART THERAPY COLORING

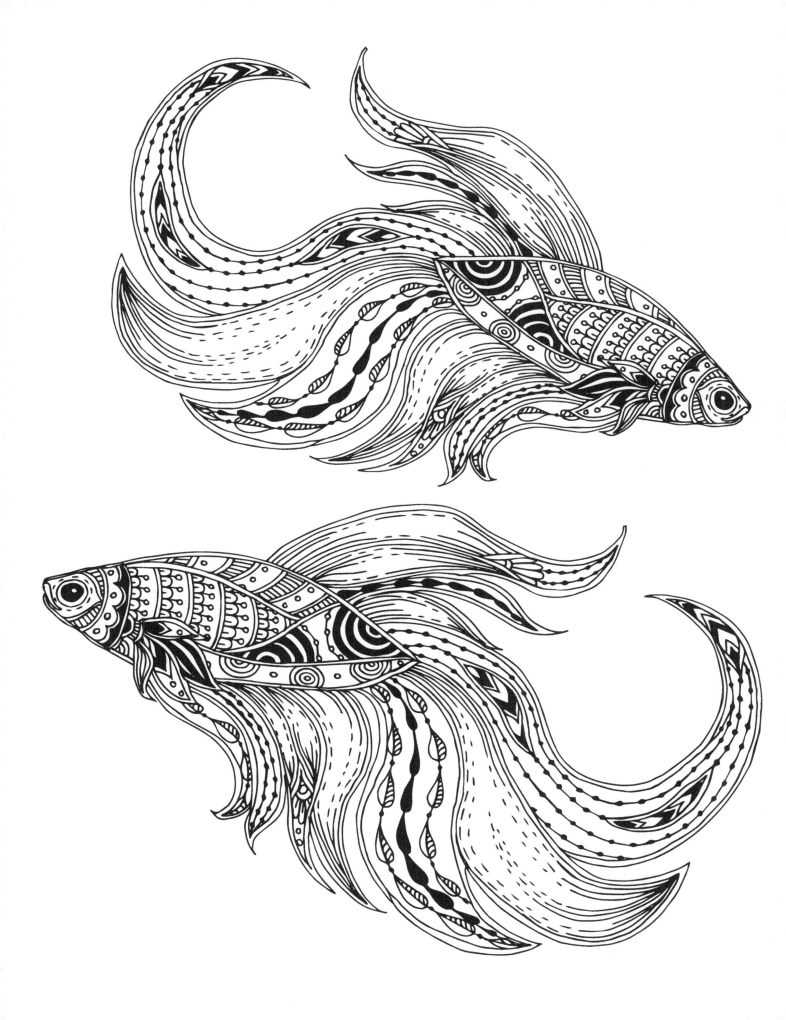

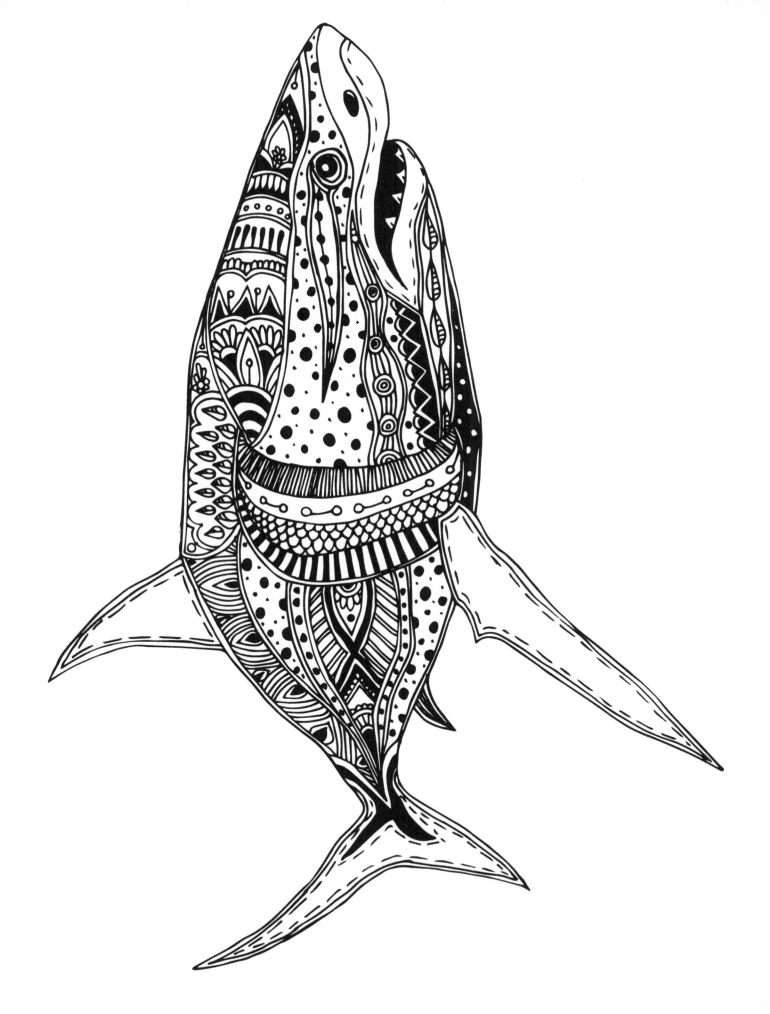

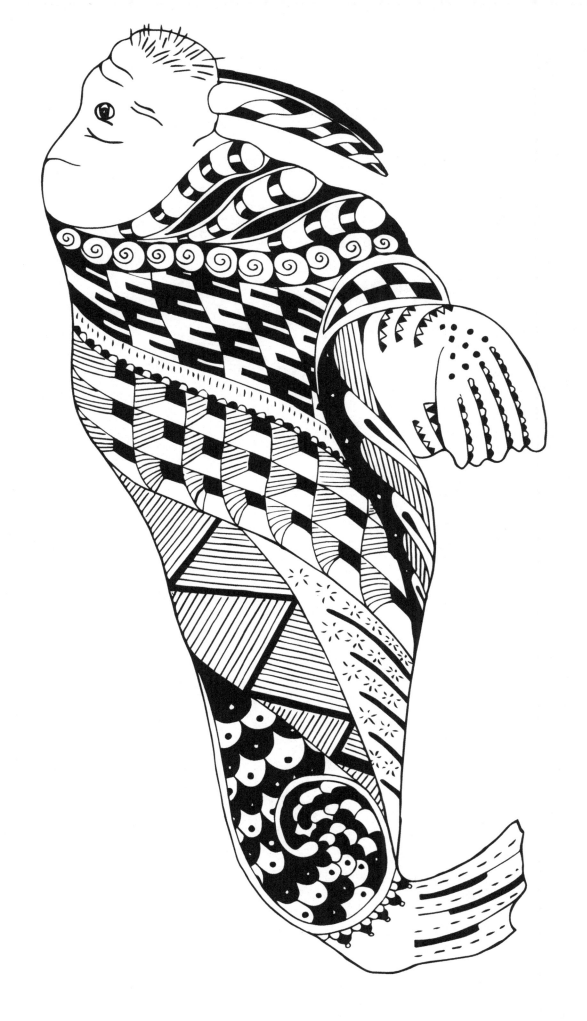

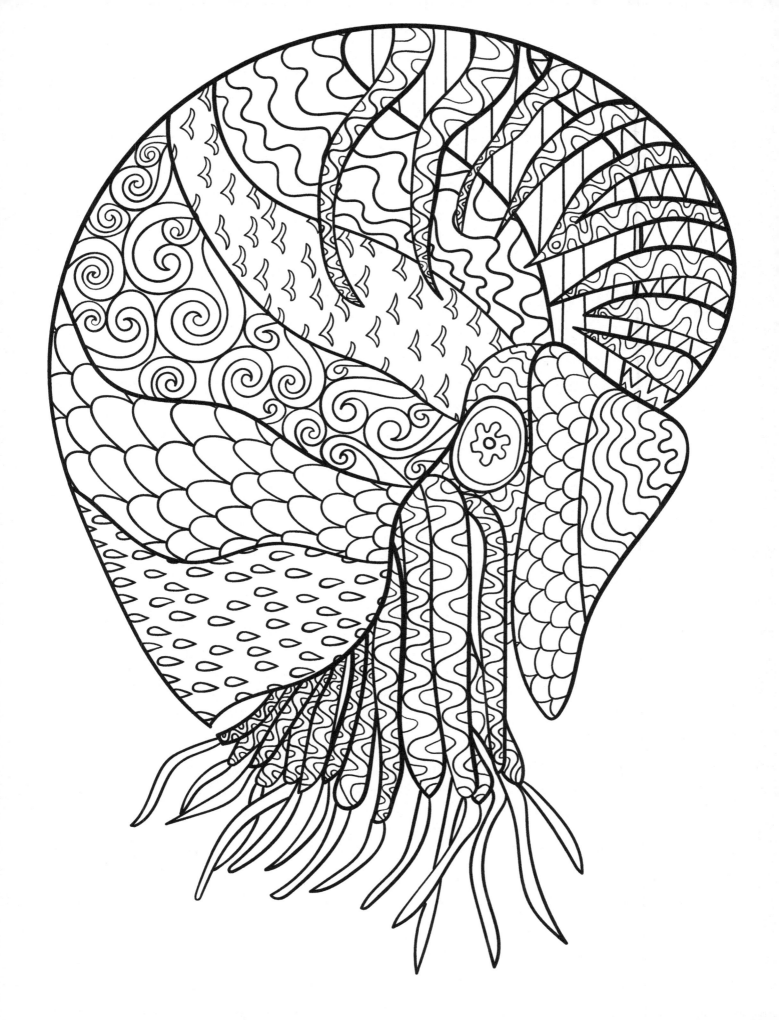

Best Selling Art Therapy Coloring Books

Coloring Books For Adults:

- Zombie Coloring Book: Black Background
- Butterfly Coloring Book For Adults: Black Background
- Tattoo Coloring Book: Black Background
- Coloring Books for Adults Relaxation: Native American Inspired Designs
- Fishing Coloring Book for Adults: Black Background

Coloring Books For Men:

- Coloring Book for Men: Anti-Stress Designs Vol 1
- Coloring Book For Men: Fishing Designs
- Coloring Book For Men: Tattoo Designs
- Coloring Books for Men: Hunting
- Coloring Book For Men: Biker Designs

Coloring Books For Seniors:

- Coloring Book For Seniors: Nature Designs Vol 1
- Coloring Book For Seniors: Anti-Stress Designs Vol 1
- Coloring Books for Seniors: Relaxing Designs
- Coloring Book For Seniors: Floral Designs Vol 1
- Coloring Book For Seniors: Ocean Designs Vol 1

Coloring Books For Teens and Tweens:

- Coloring Books For Teens: Ocean Designs
- Coloring Books for Teen Girls Vol 1
- Teen Inspirational Coloring Books
- Coloring Book for Teens: Anti-Stress Designs Vol 1
- Tween Coloring Books For Girls: Cute Animals

Coloring Books For Kids:

- Horse Coloring Book For Girls
- Coloring Books For Boys: Sharks
- Coloring Books for Boys: Animal Designs
- Unicorn Coloring Book for Girls
- Detailed Coloring Books For Kids

Art Therapy Coloring Books

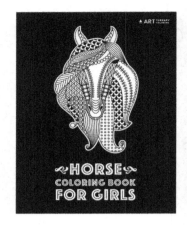

HORSE
COLORING BOOK
FOR GIRLS

UNICORN
COLORING BOOK
FOR GIRLS

COLORING
BOOKS FOR GIRLS
UNICORNS

COLORING BOOKS
FOR GIRLS
ANIMAL DESIGNS

COLORING BOOKS
FOR TEEN GIRLS VOL 1
DETAILED DESIGNS

TEEN
COLORING BOOKS
FOR GIRLS VOL 1

TEEN
COLORING BOOKS
FOR GIRLS VOL 2

TEEN
COLORING BOOKS
FOR GIRLS VOL 3

COLORING
BOOKS FOR GIRLS
CUTE ANIMALS

GIRLS
COLORING BOOKS
CUTE ANIMALS

COLORING
BOOKS FOR GIRLS
ANIMALS

COLORING BOOKS
FOR GIRLS
Princess & Unicorn Designs

GIRLS
COLORING BOOKS
DETAILED DESIGNS VOL 1

COLORING BOOKS
FOR GIRLS
DETAILED DESIGNS VOL 2

GIRLS
COLORING BOOKS
DETAILED DESIGNS VOL 2

COLORING BOOKS
FOR GIRLS
RELAXATION
Hearts

Art Therapy Coloring Books

COLORING BOOKS
FOR TEENS
WOLVES & MORE

~TEEN~
COLORING BOOKS
ANIMAL DESIGNS

~TEEN~
COLORING BOOKS
ANIMALS
Black Background

COLORING BOOKS
FOR TEENS
~ OWLS ~

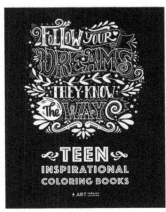

~TEEN~
INSPIRATIONAL
COLORING BOOKS

~TEEN~
COLORING BOOKS
ANIMAL DESIGNS
Black Background

~DETAILED~
COLORING BOOK
FOR TEENAGERS
Animal Designs

~TEEN~
COLORING BOOK
INSPIRATIONAL QUOTES

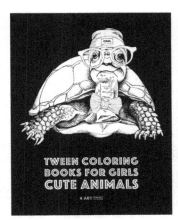

TWEEN COLORING
BOOKS FOR GIRLS
CUTE ANIMALS

ADULT COLORING BOOKS
~ FOR TEENS ~
Animal Designs

COLORING BOOKS
FOR TEENS
CAT & DOG DESIGNS

MANDALA
COLORING BOOK
FOR TEENS
Black Background

COLORING BOOKS
FOR TEENS
SEAHORSES & MORE

COLORING BOOKS
FOR TEENS
RELAXATION
Dolphins & More

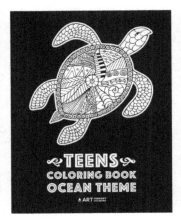

~TEENS~
COLORING BOOK
OCEAN THEME

COLORING BOOKS
FOR TEENS
SHARKS & MORE

Art Therapy Coloring Books

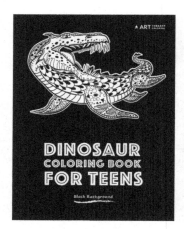

DINOSAUR
COLORING BOOK
FOR TEENS
Black Background

ANIMAL
COLORING BOOK
FOR TEENS VOL 1

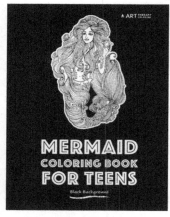

OCEAN
COLORING BOOK
ZENDOODLE DESIGNS

MERMAID
COLORING BOOK
FOR TEENS
Black Background

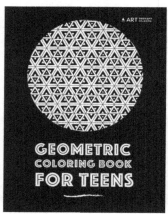

GEOMETRIC
COLORING BOOK
FOR TEENS

SKULL
COLORING BOOK
FOR TEENS
Black Background

ANIMAL
COLORING BOOK
FOR TEENS VOL 2

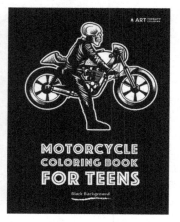

MOTORCYCLE
COLORING BOOK
FOR TEENS
Black Background

Tween Coloring Books For Girls
Black Background Vol 1

Tween Coloring Book
Black Background Vol 1

Coloring Book For Tweens
Black Background Hearts

THE ISLAND LIFE

Coloring Book For Tweens
Ocean Patterns Vol 2

Tween Coloring Book
Skull Designs

Tween Coloring Book
Mermaid & Ocean Designs

Tween Coloring Book
Ocean, Pirate, Skulls

Coloring Book For Tweens
Ocean Patterns Vol 1

Art Therapy Coloring Books

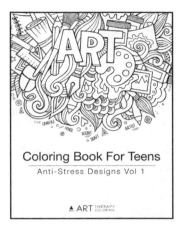

Coloring Book For Teens
Anti-Stress Designs Vol 1

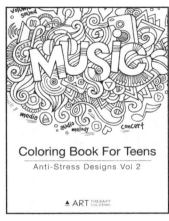

Coloring Book For Teens
Anti-Stress Designs Vol 2

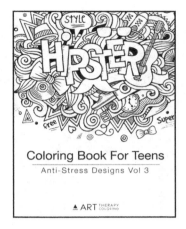

Coloring Book For Teens
Anti-Stress Designs Vol 3

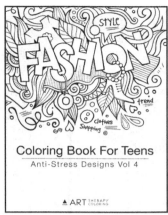

Coloring Book For Teens
Anti-Stress Designs Vol 4

Coloring Book For Teens
Anti-Stress Designs Vol 5

Coloring Book For Teens
Anti-Stress Designs Vol 6

Coloring Book For Teens
Anti-Stress Designs Vol 7

Coloring Book For Teens
Anti-Stress Designs Vol 8

Teen Coloring Book
Stress Relieving Designs

Tween Coloring Book
Animal Designs Vol 1
Stay Wild!

Tween Coloring Book
Animal Designs Vol 2

Tween Coloring Books For Girls
Stress Relief Vol 1

Tween Coloring Books For Girls
Stress Relief Vol 2

Tween Coloring Book
I Love You!!!

Tween Coloring Book
Wolves, Lions, Tigers

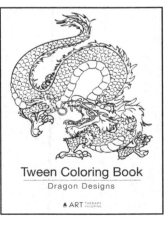

Tween Coloring Book
Dragon Designs

Art Therapy Coloring Books

COLORING BOOKS
FOR BOYS
WILD ANIMALS
ART THERAPY COLORING

COLORING BOOKS
FOR BOYS
DRAGONS
ART THERAPY COLORING

COLORING BOOKS
FOR BOYS
ANIMAL DESIGNS
ART THERAPY COLORING

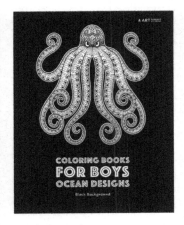

COLORING BOOKS
FOR BOYS
OCEAN DESIGNS
Black Background

COLORING BOOKS
FOR BOYS
SHARKS
ART THERAPY COLORING

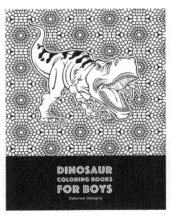

DINOSAUR
COLORING BOOKS
FOR BOYS
Detailed Designs

COLORING BOOKS
FOR BOYS
NATIVE AMERICAN INSPIRED
ART THERAPY COLORING

COLORING
BOOKS FOR BOYS
ANIMALS
ART THERAPY COLORING

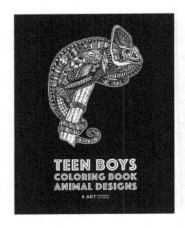

TEEN BOYS
COLORING BOOK
ANIMAL DESIGNS
ART THERAPY COLORING

TEEN COLORING BOOKS
FOR BOYS
DETAILED DESIGNS
ART THERAPY COLORING

TEEN COLORING BOOKS
FOR BOYS
DETAILED DESIGNS
Black Background

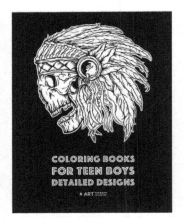

COLORING BOOKS
FOR TEEN BOYS
DETAILED DESIGNS

COLORING BOOKS
FOR TEEN BOYS
DETAILED DESIGNS
Black Background

ADULT
COLORING BOOKS
FOR KIDS
Geometric Designs

ROBOT
COLORING BOOK
DETAILED DESIGNS

DETAILED
COLORING BOOKS
FOR KIDS
Geometric Designs

Art Therapy Coloring Books

COLORING BOOKS FOR TEEN GIRLS DETAILED DESIGNS
Black Background

TEEN GIRLS COLORING BOOKS DETAILED DESIGNS
Native American Inspired

COLORING BOOKS FOR TEENS RELAXATION
Nature Designs

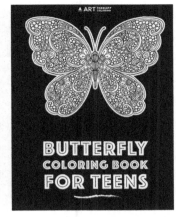

BUTTERFLY COLORING BOOK FOR TEENS

COLORING BOOKS FOR TEEN GIRLS VOL 2 DETAILED DESIGNS

ADULT COLORING BOOKS FOR GIRLS
Detailed Designs

COLORING BOOKS FOR GIRLS DETAILED DESIGNS VOL 1

COLORING BOOKS FOR GIRLS OCEAN DESIGNS

COLORING BOOKS FOR GIRLS RELAXATION
Black Background

COLORING BOOKS FOR OLDER KIDS GEOMETRIC DESIGNS

HEART COLORING BOOK FOR KIDS

DETAILED COLORING BOOKS FOR KIDS
Ocean Designs

ANIMAL COLORING BOOK FOR OLDER KIDS

COLORING BOOKS FOR OLDER KIDS ANIMAL DESIGNS

COLORING BOOKS FOR GIRLS RELAXATION
Butterflies

BUTTERFLY COLORING BOOK FOR KIDS
Detailed Designs

Art Therapy Coloring Books

DETAILED COLORING BOOKS FOR KIDS
Zoo Animals

COLORING BOOKS FOR KIDS AGES 8-12 ANIMALS
Black Background

DETAILED COLORING BOOKS FOR KIDS

ZOMBIE COLORING BOOK FOR KIDS

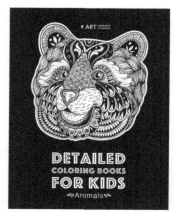

DETAILED COLORING BOOKS FOR KIDS
Animals

DETAILED COLORING BOOKS FOR KIDS
Elephants

COLORING BOOKS FOR KIDS OCEAN DESIGNS

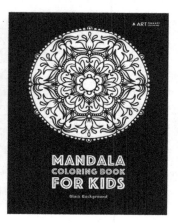

MANDALA COLORING BOOK FOR KIDS
Black Background

DETAILED COLORING BOOKS FOR KIDS
Butterflies

UNICORN COLORING BOOK FOR KIDS AGES 4-8
Volume 1

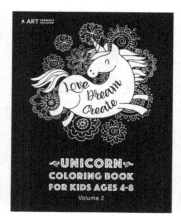

UNICORN COLORING BOOK FOR KIDS AGES 4-8
Volume 2

COLORING BOOKS FOR KIDS CUTE ANIMALS

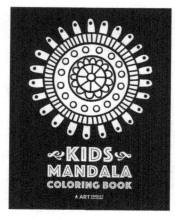

KIDS MANDALA COLORING BOOK

MANDALA COLORING BOOK FOR KIDS

SHARK COLORING BOOK

DINOSAUR COLORING BOOK

Art Therapy Coloring Books

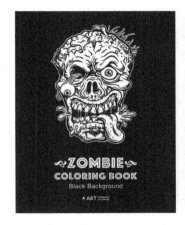

ZOMBIE
COLORING BOOK
Black Background

ZOMBIES
COLORING BOOK
SCARY DESIGNS
Black Background

DRAGON
COLORING BOOK

WOLF
COLORING BOOK
FOR ADULTS

AFRICA
COLORING BOOK
FOR ADULTS

LION
COLORING BOOK
FOR ADULTS

TIGER
COLORING BOOK
FOR ADULTS

WILD ANIMALS
COLORING BOOK
ZENDOODLE DESIGNS

MERRY
CHRISTMAS
AND HAPPY NEW YEAR

CHRISTMAS
COLORING BOOK
FOR TEENS
Black Background

UNICORN
ADULT COLORING BOOKS
Black Background

HORSE
COLORING BOOKS
FOR ADULTS
Black Background

CUTE ANIMAL
COLORING BOOK

Christmas Coloring Book For Kids
Black Background Designs
& Gratitude Journal

MERRY
CHRISTMAS

Christmas Coloring Book For Kids
Detailed Designs Vol 1

Ho, Ho, Ho,
Y'all!

Christmas Coloring Book For Kids
Detailed Designs Vol 2

Christmas Coloring Book For Kids
Detailed Festive Designs

Coloring Books & Gratitude Journals In One

Gratitude Journal & Coloring Book

For Older Kids: Animals & Inspiration
Black Background Designs

Gratitude Journal & Coloring Book

For Older Kids: Animal Designs & Inspiration

ART THERAPY COLORING

Gratitude Journal & Coloring Book

For Older Kids: Animals & Inspiration

ART THERAPY COLORING

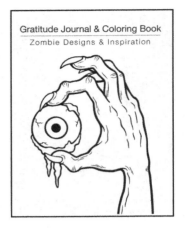

Gratitude Journal & Coloring Book

Zombie Designs & Inspiration

Coloring Book For Older Kids

Animals & Gratitude Journal Vol 1

ART THERAPY COLORING

Coloring Book For Older Kids

Animals & Gratitude Journal Vol 2

ART THERAPY COLORING

Coloring Book For Older Kids

Birds & Gratitude Journal

ART THERAPY COLORING

Coloring Books For Older Kids

Animals & Gratitude Journal

ART THERAPY COLORING

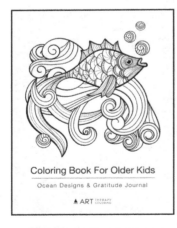

Coloring Book For Older Kids

Ocean Designs & Gratitude Journal

ART THERAPY COLORING

Coloring Book For Older Kids

Animals & Gratitude Journal Vol 3

ART THERAPY COLORING

Coloring Book For Tweens

Ocean Designs & Gratitude Journal

ART THERAPY COLORING

Robot Coloring Book

& Gratitude Journal

ART THERAPY COLORING

Gratitude Journal & Coloring Book

Dragons: Black Background Designs

ART

Coloring Book For Older Kids

Midnight Space Designs
& Gratitude Journal

Tween Coloring Books For Girls

Black Background Designs
& Gratitude Journal

ART

Teen Gratitude Journal & Coloring Book

Cute Animal Designs
Black Background

ART

Coloring Books & Gratitude Journals In One

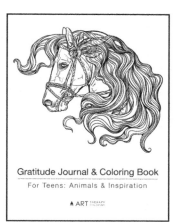

Gratitude Journal & Coloring Book

For Teens: Animals & Inspiration

▲ ART THERAPY COLORING

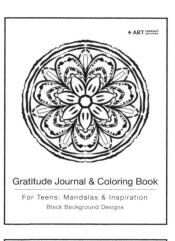

Gratitude Journal & Coloring Book

For Teens: Mandalas & Inspiration
Black Background Designs

Gratitude Journal & Coloring Book

For Teens: Fairies & Inspiration

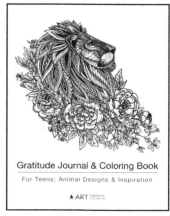

Gratitude Journal & Coloring Book

For Teens: Animal Designs & Inspiration

▲ ART THERAPY COLORING

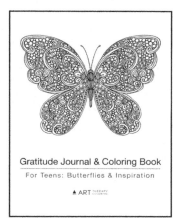

Gratitude Journal & Coloring Book

For Teens: Butterflies & Inspiration

▲ ART THERAPY COLORING

Gratitude Journal & Coloring Book

For Tweens: Dog Doodles & Inspiration

▲ ART THERAPY COLORING

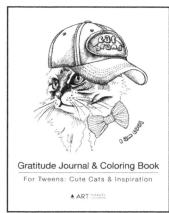

Gratitude Journal & Coloring Book

For Tweens: Cute Cats & Inspiration

▲ ART THERAPY COLORING

Gratitude Journal & Coloring Book

For Girls: Cute Animals & Inspiration

▲ ART THERAPY COLORING

Gratitude Journal & Coloring Book

For Girls: Butterflies & Inspiration

▲ ART THERAPY COLORING

Gratitude Journal & Coloring Book

For Girls: Birds & Inspiration

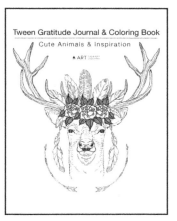

Tween Gratitude Journal & Coloring Book

Cute Animals & Inspiration

▲ ART THERAPY COLORING

Tween Coloring Books For Girls

Hearts & Gratitude Journal

▲ ART THERAPY COLORING

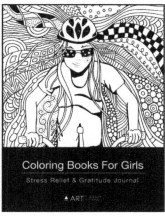

Coloring Books For Girls

Stress Relief & Gratitude Journal

▲ ART THERAPY COLORING

Tween Coloring Books For Girls

Cute Animals & Gratitude Journal

▲ ART THERAPY COLORING

Coloring Books For Girls Vol 1

Cute Animals & Gratitude Journal

▲ ART THERAPY COLORING

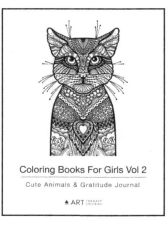

Coloring Books For Girls Vol 2

Cute Animals & Gratitude Journal

▲ ART THERAPY COLORING

Coloring Books For Teens
Ocean Designs

Published by:
Art Therapy Coloring
www.arttherapycoloring.com

Shutterstock Images

ISBN: 978-1-64126-055-8

Made in the USA
Monee, IL
15 April 2020